Art to make you smile

Elizabeth Newbery

F

FRANCES LINCOLN
CHILDREN'S BOOKS

The happy elephant

A white elephant is a very rare animal. It's so special that in ancient Thailand, even kings were not allowed to ride on it. White elephants were not allowed to work, so they were very expensive to keep. They cost so much money to look after, that one king gave a white elephant to a nobleman he didn't like – knowing that he would go broke.

This white elephant is very happy. It smiles as servants fuss around preparing its bath. It likes having its back scrubbed.

Watch out, we might get wet!

I've never seen a white elephant before!

A White Elephant is embroidered on to blue silk. It was made in Japan about 200 years ago.

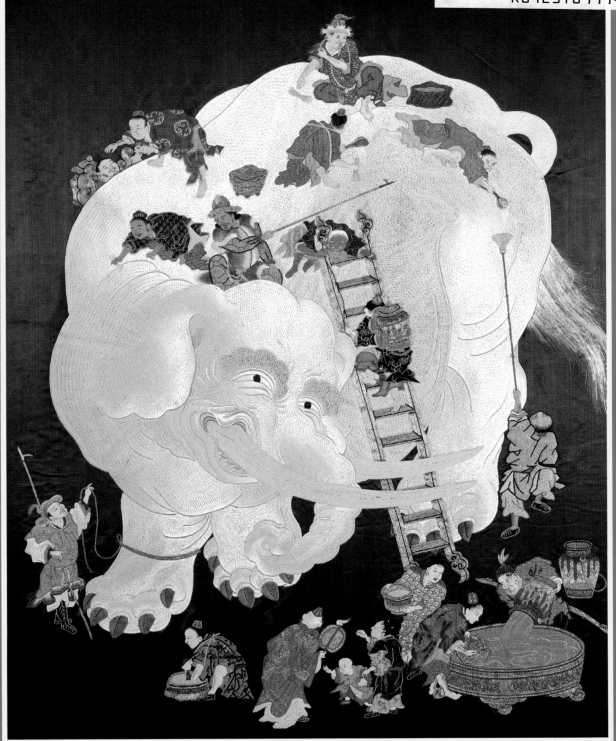

Cheeky monkey

Have you seen a mandrill in a zoo? They are those large, colourful baboons with white cheeks, yellow beards, red noses and blue bottoms! No wonder Oskar Kokoschka wanted to paint this one that lived in the monkey house at London Zoo.

The Mandrill looks as though it is GRINNING doesn't it? But Oskar was quite sure the mandrill hated him – even though he always took it a banana.

Let's give it a banana!

Perhaps it doesn't like bananas.

Let's dress up!

Sir Joshua Reynolds lived about 250 years ago. He painted portraits of rich men and women and their children. This is a portrait of Master John Crewe aged 4. He was the eldest son of Lord and Lady Crewe.

Little John Crewe is wearing a fancy dress costume modelled on a famous old picture of King Henry VIII. What fun it must have been to have such beautiful dressing-up clothes!

Can you see John's green everyday coat on the chair beside him? And one of his little pet King Charles spaniels, sniffing curiously around his master's strange clothes?

I'm going to dress up as a king too.

DRESSING UP BOX

8

Master Crewe as Henry VIII was painted by Sir Joshua Reynolds in 1776.

A chair with a face

Most of the artists in this book learnt how to draw, paint and make things in art schools or in the studios of other artists. But Richard Dial, who made this chair, worked in a car factory in America.

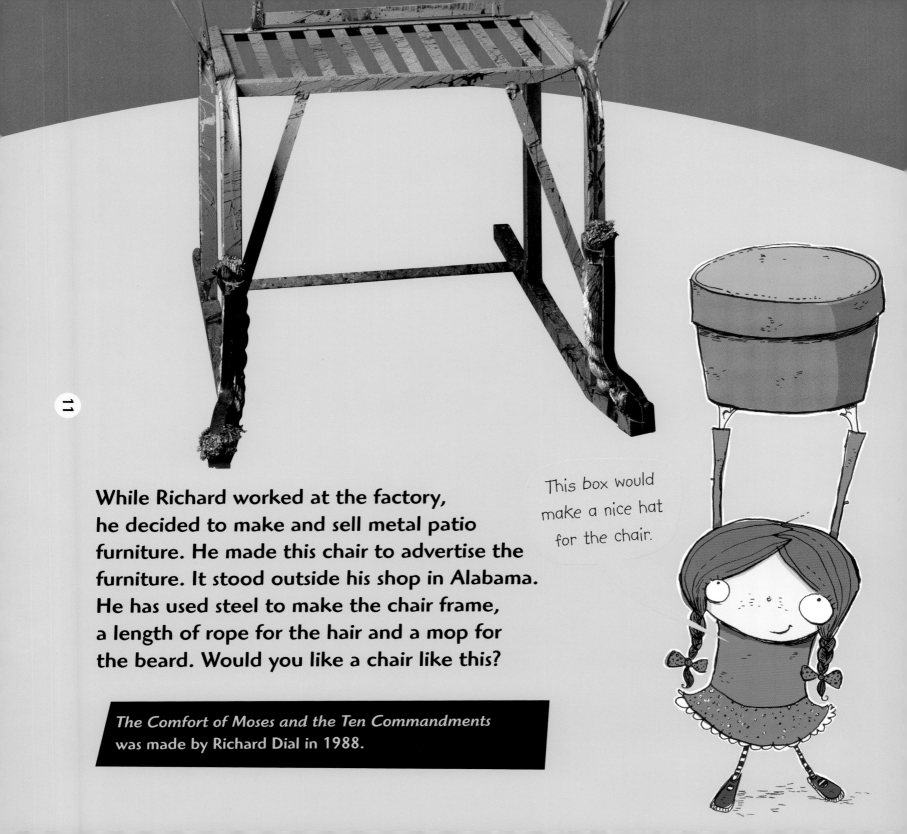

While Richard worked at the factory, he decided to make and sell metal patio furniture. He made this chair to advertise the furniture. It stood outside his shop in Alabama. He has used steel to make the chair frame, a length of rope for the hair and a mop for the beard. Would you like a chair like this?

The Comfort of Moses and the Ten Commandments was made by Richard Dial in 1988.

This box would make a nice hat for the chair.

Dogs at work

Have you got a pet? Perhaps you imagine that sometimes it looks sad, cross or happy. Well, Sir Edwin Landseer, who painted this picture, decided to have a bit of fun and paint dogs with human expressions. Some people think the dogs were modelled on his friends!

Landseer has pretended the dogs are taking part in a trial. The big fluffy poodle is the judge wearing a white wig, and a trusty black retriever has the important documents. A terrier glances up eagerly and a spaniel looks bored. A wolfhound turns to whisper something to a wise old bloodhound. What do you think it's saying?

Oh gosh, he looks like me now!

Laying Down The Law was painted by Sir Edward Landseer in 1840.

A BIG grin

This man sits with his legs crossed and his left hand raised as if to say, "I'm plotting something". He is wearing a mask with a huge GRIN. Who is he?

His mask shows that he is an actor who performed in popular plays in Ancient Greece. The grin tells us he took part in comedies with **rude jokes** and lots of **fooling around**. So he is probably plotting some mischief!

He he he he he!

14

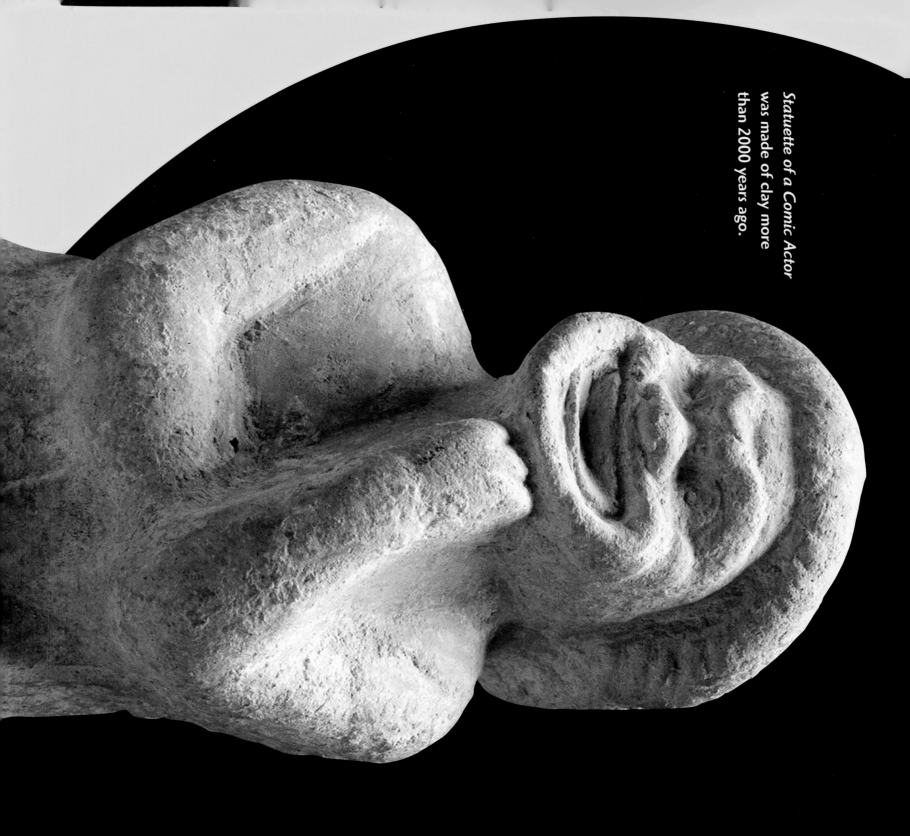

Statuette of a Comic Actor was made of clay more than 2000 years ago.

The snowball fight

These two cheeky boys look as though they're having a wonderful time in the snow, don't they? There are bits of snow on the boy's jacket on the left. Perhaps the boy on the right has just hit him with a snowball. But now the boys look as though they are ganging up and about to aim snowballs at the photographer. Do you think they'll get him?

Let's get him!

Snowballers, Bethnal Green was photographed by Roger Mayne in 1955.

Roger Mayne, the photographer, took lots of photos of children when he went to live in London after the Second World War. This photo was taken in Bethnal Green, in the east end of London.

A monster cheeseburger

Claes Oldenburg is an American sculptor. He gets ideas from ordinary things such as plugs and switches, petrol pumps, ping-pong tables and food – especially fast food. He plays around with the size to make ENORMOUS slices of cake and ice creams, HUGE sandwiches and hamburgers and GIANT lollipops.

Yum, I want one!

Corr, they look scrummy!

18

These jumbo cheeseburgers are made
of stuffed canvas and painted plaster.
Would YOU like to eat that?

Two Cheeseburgers was made by
Claes Oldenburg in 1962.

More about the art and artists

● **The White Elephant** is embroidered in silk thread on to blue silk. You can see it in the Victoria and Albert Museum, London. Sadly we don't know the people who embroidered it, but we can tell that they were very skilful.

● **The Mandrill** by Oskar Kokoschka is painted in oil paints. *The Mandrill* can be seen in Museum Boymans van Beuningen in Rotterdam.

Oskar Kokoschka was born in Austria in 1886 and died in 1980. At school he wanted to study chemistry, but when his teacher saw Oskar's wonderful drawings, he told him to study art instead.

Later, Oskar was seriously wounded in the First World War. After his wounds had healed he travelled all over Europe, North Africa, Egypt, Turkey, Palestine and to England where he painted *The Mandrill*.

● **Master Crewe as Henry VIII** is painted by **Sir Joshua Reynolds** in oil paints. It is in a private collection.

Sir Joshua Reynolds was born in 1723 and died in 1792. His father was a headmaster and saw to it that young Joshua was well educated. Joshua became great friends with the celebrities of his day. By the time he died, he had painted the portraits of almost every important man and woman living at that time.

● **Richard Dial** made *The Comfort of Moses and the Ten Commandments.* You can see it in the American Folk Art Museum, New York.

A long time ago, many people couldn't read or write. Shopkeepers put large figures and signs outside their shops to show what they were selling. You can still see some old shop signs in towns, although they usually hang above shops. This chair is only about 20 years old so although it was put together to advertise Richard Dial's shop, it was made mainly for fun.

● *Laying Down The Law* by Sir Edwin Landseer is painted in oil paints. You can see it in Chatsworth House in Derbyshire.

Sir Edwin Landseer was born in 1802 and died in 1873. He was a brilliant animal painter and his paintings were very popular in Victorian times. In fact, he was Queen Victoria's favourite painter! But his most famous work of art is not a painting at all. It's the four great lions at the bottom of Nelson's Column in Trafalgar Square, London.

● *Statuette of a Comic Actor*
This little clay statuette is only about 10 centimetres (4 inches) high. We don't know who made it but we do know it was made between 325-275 BC in Ancient Greece. Today, you can see it in the J. Paul Getty Museum in Los Angeles.

Statuettes of famous actors were popular knick-knacks in Ancient Greece. Some people think that they were bought in sets so that they could be put together to make scenes from famous plays.

● *Roger Mayne* photographed *Snowballers, Bethnal Green* in 1955. Many of his photographs, including *Snowballers, Bethnal Green* are in the Victoria and Albert Museum, London.

Roger Mayne was born in 1929. He took the photograph of *Snowballers, Bethnal Green* 50 years ago. Many children were allowed to play out in the street then. There were fewer cars so it wasn't as dangerous as it is today.

● *Two Cheeseburgers* by Claes Oldenburg can be seen in the Museum of Modern Art, New York.

Claes Oldenburg was born in 1929. Most sculptors make sculptures out of hard materials such as plaster, bronze or fired clay. Claes Oldenburg makes his sculptures out of soft materials that droop, sag or sway.

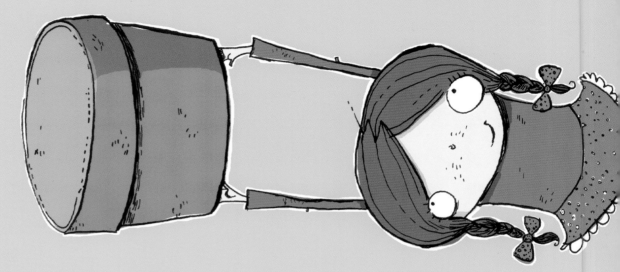

PHOTOGRAPHIC ACKNOWLEDGMENTS

For permission to reproduce the works of art shown on the following pages and for supplying images, the Publishers would like to thank:
Collection American Folk Art Museum, New York. (Purchase made possible with grants from the National Endowment for the Arts and the Metropolitan Life Foundation). 1990.3.5. Photo by Bard Wrisley: front cover (detail) and 10–11
© The Devonshire Collection, Chatsworth. (Reproduced by permission of the Chatsworth Settlement Trustees): 12
J. Paul Getty Museum, Los Angeles (96.AD.164): 14–15
Museum Boymans van Beuningen, Rotterdam, The Netherlands/
The Bridgeman Art Library/© DACS 2007: 6–7
Digital image © 2005 The Museum of Modern Art, New York/Scala, Florence. Philip Johnson Fund. 233.1962/sculpture © Claes Oldenburg and Coosje van Bruggen: 18–19
Private Collection: 9
V&A Images/Victoria and Albert Museum: 5
V&A Images/Victoria and Albert Museum/© Roger Mayne: 16–17

Art to Make You Smile copyright
© Frances Lincoln Limited 2007
Text copyright © Elizabeth Newbery 2007

Designed by Rachel Hamdi/Holly Fulbrook
Special illustrations by Sarah Horne

First published in Great Britain in 2007 and in the USA in 2008
by Frances Lincoln Children's Books,
4 Torriano Mews, Torriano Avenue, London NW5 2RZ
www.franceslincoln.com

British Library Cataloguing in Publication Data available on request

ISBN: 978-1-84507-583-5

Printed in Singapore

9 8 7 6 5 4 3 2 1